Righteous Reflections

By

Dennis J. Gibbons

First Published in 2000 by Words & Phrases, 2231 South 14th Street, La Crosse, Wisconsin 54601

ISBN: 0 75965 236 8

This book is printed on acid free paper.

1stBooks - rev. 06/29/01

There is no path. You make the path you walk

Antonio Machado

Table of Contents

Introduction

Millenium

Part I - The Good, The Sad, And The Ugly

"I'm Such A Macho Guy" ... 3
"I'm A Liberated Woman' ... 4
Good Advice ... 5
The Next Generation ... 6
If Everyone Got Their Act Together ... 7
The Terror Of the Mall ... 8
Mall Daze ... 9
The Day ... 10
Giving Advice ... 11
People Don't Like Me ... 12
Third Generation ... 13
Some People From Wisconsin ... 14
You Claim To Have The Answers ... 15
Why Do People? ... 16
IT ... 17
Why Should 1 Be Nervous? ... 18
Don't Think It Can Happen? ... 19
Unwelcome To Our Town ... 20
Somewhere ... 21
Vets ... 22
The C Word ... 23
You Must Have Had ... 24
An Honest Man ... 25
Some People ... 26

Millenium Georgey 27
Politically Correct 28
Sixties Syndrome 29
They're Everywhere! 30
Poor People 31
Liberal La La Land 32
My Father's War 33
Why Do Seniors? 34

Part II - Sentimental Journey

Know Who You Are 37
When You Say It 38
The Moment 39
Why Can't I? 40
Before You - Since You 41
Since You 42
Stilted 43
What Was I Thinking? 44
The Parking Lot At K- Mart 45
So Sorry 46
Some Guy 48
You Are More 49
Like Number 20 50
When You Look At Me 51
Don't Cling To Me 52
The Ride 53
Did You Ride? 54
Said A Prayer 55
Why Is It? 56
Don't Think 57

If I Could Have Met You Sooner 58
The Stranger 59
Finally 60
A Bitter Poem 61
She Smiled 62
Part III - Love And Family
The Magical Place 65
Mikey Swings 67
Why Do People Love Them? 68
Being A Grandparent 69
Instead Gave Me 70
The Baby Did This 71
You Say 72
House And Not a Home 73
A Message To My Son 74
When I Was Young 76
Part IV - Alcohol And The Night
Said I Was Your Brother 79
"A Lot Of Ouestions" 80
One Is Too Many 81
The Stalker 82
Through Our Daughter 83
Let The Monster Sleep 84
Still Waiting 85
The Roughest Bar In Town 86
Walking On Eggshells 87
Believed You 88
Looking For A Quiet Place 89
Whacked Out 91

Why Do People Drink? 92
Little Girl 93
Sailor's Goodbye 95

Introduction

Many of you who have read my previous books will be surprised by the context of this one. Righteous Reflections does contain a lot about romance, relationships and the night life, however, it also reflects social, political and religious themes.

I want to make it clear. I am not against the government, the police, religion or social drinking. I am concerned about government influence, abuse of police power, religious hypocrisy, cruel and irresponsible behavior brought on by alcohol, selfishness, lust for power and just plain meaness.

As I stated in The Light And The Dark, "I'm a social observer not a social critic." Words can inform and entertain, but words can also hurt. Someone once said to me, "Dennis, some of your writing is sentimental sweet and some of it is "kick in the FACE mean." I apologize now. Righteous Reflections is a compilation of how I sometimes view people and situations based on observations, feelings and imagination.

Dennis Gibbons
LaCrosse, Wisconsin
2000

Millenium

A century has ended and a new millenium has begun, We look back at the Twentieth Century with mixed feelings. To paraphrase Charles Dickens, "It was the best and worst of times." Two World Wars and many smaller wars. A major holocaust; and many other examples of man's inhumanity to man on a massive scale. The last half-century we've had the potential to completely destroy ourselves.

On the other hand. we have seen the defeat of many totalitarian states, and an improved quality of life for many. We can now expect to live twice as long as people did a century before. Technology has been a blessing and a curse. Our enviroment has changed significantly and our pace has accelerated.

We are still like our ancestors in many ways. We still have our hopes and dreams and our fears and regrets. We should never give up trying to make our world a better place.

We must be optimistic, but vigilant. Hopefully, those in power will govern justly. Political and social institutions will guide with reason and compassion, and we as individuals will learn to treat each other better. Instead of fearing the system, we can benefit from it, and give back.

We can overcome our fears and prejudices. Replace fear with trust, conquer hate with love, defeat ignorance with knowledge and proceed with brave confident steps into the new millenium.

Part I.

The Good, The Sad, And The Ugly

"I'm Such A Macho Guy"

I'm such a macho guy
Not a well-mannered fool
Don't wear a coat in winter
So "chicks" will think I'm cool

Don't have a hernia
Force myself to walk this way
Shout and swear, when I talk
So no one thinks I'm gay

Can't speak about women
Without a coarse word or two
Cause women are not people
And I'm macho and I'm cool

Never outgrew it
Search for it every night
Find someone half my size
Try to start a fight

Sensitivity is for losers
Hurting others is a joy
I'm really not so macho
I'm a selfish, little boy

"I'm A Liberated Woman'

I'm a liberated woman
Oh, can't you see
Took a course in women's studies
Now, I'm really free

I'm so liberated
Self-reliant and strong
Handle any problem
Right any wrong

Embrace any cause
You can't call me frail
Love every minority
Want to save the whale!

Can drink and swear
More than most men do
Dress like a slob-drive reckless
Cause I'm liberated and so cool!

When its not to my benefit
Give feminism a rest
Turn on "the sprinkler system"
Arch my back-stick out my chest

When the clock is striking thirty
And my body starts to sag
I' 11 tire of foolish games
Find life quite a drag

Give up my independence
No longer feel so free
Find a guy with lots of dough
To take good care of me

Good Advice

We all obtain some wisdom
Somewhere along in life
If you heed these words
You will avoid some strife

Don't argue with the cops
Those filled up on booze
Women, trains or semis
For you are sure to lose

The Next Generation

Since the 1950's, they've had
The luxury to rebel
Teenagers have found so many ways
To make their parents yell

Duck tails and Elvis
Bell-bottoms and died shirts
Hippie-hair and sandals
Shaved heads and miniskirts

I'm not an old conservative
I also did rebel
My hair, music, and clothing
Made my parents yell

But this latest generation
Searching for who they are
In my opinion have pushed things
A little bit too far

Covered with tattoos
Obscenities on clothes
Claiming to worship the devil
An earing in the nose

What will the next generation do
To top the present one
Drive their parents crazy
Have a lot of fun?

Perhaps girls will wear dresses
The boys a shirt and tie
Crew-cuts and beehives
The flag and apple pie

If Everyone Got Their Act Together

If everyone got their act together
What a boring world it would be
Not to mention the affect
on the economy

Cops would lose their jobs
Jailors would too
Counselors and social workers
Wouldn't have much to do

Liquor stores would lose business
So would every bar
There would be layoffs
At every hospital E.R.

When we do something bad
Or feel a first-class clown
To feel good about ourselves
On who would we look down!

The Terror Of the Mall

They teased him back in school
Called him "fatso" and "a tard"
No wonder he chose a career
As a security guard

Wants to mess with people
Never got his G.E.D.
Lives in his parent's basement
Plays on his C.B.

Uniform ill-fitting
Belly to the knees
Walks with a swagger
Trails a string of keys

Wisely armed him with a flashlight
And a two-way radio
Feared he'd shoot someone
Or blow off his big toe

Now, he's checking license plates
Having quite a ball-'
A real-life cop "wannabee"
The terror of the mall

Mall Daze

Finally found a parking space
About a mile away
Began the trek to the stores
About a mile away

Push my way through
Howling kids and seas of gray
Feeling claustrophobic
"Get out of my way!"

Some save on babysitting
Bring along a child
Pretend they're not the parent
Let the kid run wild

Most men hate the mall
Find it boring and so hard
Mumble to themselves
"She's got my credit card"

Most women love the mall
Find it cool and oh, so keen
Must be the XX chromosome
That carries the shopping gene

Made the big mistake
Picked the shortest line
"Scanner down-price check this!"
Hear the store clerk whine

Headache building
Must get out of here
Find a quiet place
Have myself a beer

There are many types of masochists
One definition doesn't fit them all
But one must surely be
A shopper at the mall

The Day

Heard it on the radio
Felt my throat get dry
Couldn't believe it happened
Thought he would never die

My mind drifted back
To many years ago
To childhood and Saturdays
And my favorite TV show

Life was so simple then
Problems would go away
Because Roy and Dale and Gabby
Would always save the day

We knew right from wrong
The good guys always won
Families stuck together
There was no Viet Nam

And I a man of fifty
Bowed my head and cried
Felt so old and empty
The day Roy Rogers died

Giving Advice

Tell a smoker
Cigarettes are bad
I doubt he will thank you
He'll probably just get mad

Tell a heavy drinker
That he should slow down
If he doesn't curse you
He will at least reply with a frown

Tell someone obese
If they lost a lot of weight
They would like themselves more
And really feel great

And like the smoker and drinker
He will attack
Tell you to mind your business
Get off of his back

I don't give out much advice
Have problems of my own
My life is far from perfect
So I let well enough alone

People know what's wrong with them
And what they should do
But its up to them to work it out
Its not up to you

People Don't Like Me

People don't like me
Because I'm young and free
They don't like me
Because I'm old and gray

Don't like me because
I'm yellow or red
Don't like me because I'm brown
Just because I'm black
They jerk me around

Hate taking orders
Being someone's fool
That's why teachers picked on me
When I was back in school

The cops
Won't get off my back
If anyone criticizes me
I rise up and attack

It's not my fault
Try to get along
Its just that I am always right
And the rest of the world is wrong

Third Generation

Let me introduce myself
You've probably heard my name around
Although it doesn't mean a thing
Outside this one-horse town

I'm quite a success, you know
Hope I don't sound cruel
But, I have third generation money
So, I am better than you

Probably think I haven't worked a day
Afraid that you are right
Hob-nob with the elite all day
Then party through the night

Brag to impress you
But won't buy you a drink
You might think I'm cheap
But, I don't care what you think

Grandpa built the business
Father kept it around
But my drinking and attitude
Will run it in the ground

Some People From Wisconsin

Some people from Wisconsin
Drive like they're from Boston, Mass.
Swerve and cut you off
Step hard upon the gas

Some seniors drive so slow
They make you want to moan
Perhaps they are going to visit their children
At some nursing home

Some people must have spent the last decade
On Venus or Mars
Still think they can booze it up
Hop into their cars

Now, a moron dogs in front of me
While I'm trying to write this poem
Drink coffee and eat a burger
Talk on my cell-phone

If everyone drove real safe
What a great world it would be
If only everyone drove
As perfect as me

You Claim To Have The Answers

You claim to have the answers
To Heaven, Hell, and life
If I believe your every word
I will avoid much strife

Religion can make you positive
Improve the life you live
Making you loving and generous
Able to forgive

Help you over troubled waters
Heal the heart and soul
Strengthen your resolve
Clear a painful woe

But people like you
Become cold from within
Judge those around you
As if you have no sin

Now, you're trying to persuade me
With your rhetoric of dread
But even the devil can quote scripture
So, the greatest writer said

You say that Jesus loves me
Pray its really true
But why would he tell
Someone like you

Why Do People?

Why do people gamble?
Why do people drink?
The answer is quite simple
Anyway, that's what I think

Why do people smoke?
Stuff themselves with food?
Endanger their precious health
To feel a little good?

Life is hard at times
We need a little break
Do things we shouldn't
Even though its a mistake

Stress reliever is a euphemism
For a lot of vice
If we didn't have to do those things
Wouldn't it be nice?

IT

It is many things
Love and intimacy
Stress relief and fun
Can produce offspring

It can also be a weapon
They use it against us
I'm sure since Ancient times
Men have hated It

Can't go inside the feminine mind
But maybe they freeze up
When the man in their life
Has done something, or didn't do something

So, they reward us with It
Withhold It to punish
And of course
Use It to get their way

Some men react like Rhett Butler
Find their amusements elsewhere
Most men become passive-aggressive
Do more of what she dislikes

There has to be a better way
To handle such a delicate situation
Because after thousands of years
It still usually backfires

Why Should 1 Be Nervous?

Pulled up to a redlight
Came to a complete stop
In the rearview mirror
Think I see a cop

Why do I feel nervous?
Have my seatbelt on?
Don't have any weapons?
Am not an ex-con?

Haven't done a thing wrong?
Not a sleazeball?
Have a driver's license?
Haven't consumed any alcohol?

But, instead of a citizen
I feel like a mouse
And the cop appears a tomcat
Ready to make a pounce

The police don't have it easy
Have to be on their guard
Their job can be dangerous
At times rather hard

Maybe I sound paronoid
But would you answer me?
What happened to protect and serve?
America, the free?

Don't Think It Can Happen?

Forget the Magna Charta
The Petition Of Right
Tear up the Constitution
Destroy every human right

Hire another cop
Build another jail
Pass so many laws
Make us all a criminal

Say its for our protection
"Trust us, its alright"
Slowly but surely
Take another bite

Make 1984 a reality
Wouldn't that be great?
Turn our republic
Into a police state

Think it cannot happen
We might wake up someday
Living in a nightmare
Freedoms torn away

Unwelcome To Our Town

You better keep on driving
We don't want you around
We don't like strangers
So, unwelcome to our town

Love the town the way it is
It's orderly and right
The police make sure of it
Every day and night

We have our "trailer trash"
A minority or two
But we're mostly affuent
Anglo-Saxon and true-blue

Our speed limits are ridiculous
So, its easy to make a bust
The dark-skinned and out-of-town
We hold with such disgust

We hate taxi drivers
For we can't put a squeeze
O.WI.'s and fines
So, we can hire more police

We don't like teenagers
With their arrogant crap
Hanging by convenience stores
Blasting obscene rap

If you insist on hanging around
To have a little fun
We'll welcome you the way they did Stallone
Back in "Rambo One"

Somewhere

Somewhere on a Saturday
She sits by the phone
Knowing it will never ring
Another night alone

Somewhere on a barstool
Guzzles down the beers
Misses his ex-wife and children
Fight to block the tears

Somewhere in a marriage bed
Two people turn away
Fear another night
Dread another day

Somewhere with painful patience
Sits all alone
Hoping for a visitor
At the nursing home

How sad the world at times
Selfishness and despair
This thing they call loneliness
Plagues us everywhere

Vets

World War II vets were thanked
Korean vets forgotten
Viet Nam vets were scorned
Do I smell something rotten?

The C Word

The C word and the P word
What is wrong with you?
You're really disgusting
But think yourself so cool

If you don't have a daughter
You must have had a mother
I'd lecture you on respect
But, why should I bother

You're stuck in an adolescent world
That's where you will always be
Can't accept that women are people
Just like you and me

The C word and the P word
You really make me sick
No wonder I never see
You with a "chick"

You Must Have Had

You must have had a memory loss
Because down at the bar
Said you bought a new CD player
To put into your car

Now, you're buying top shelf
For the floozy by the door
Said you went to a casino
And you're going back to lose some more

Called an aplliance store
Reserved a big-screen TV
See me seethe with anger
Wonder what is wrong with me

Must have had a memory loss
Or some other mental quirk
"Where's the money you owe me
You ungrateful jerk!"

An Honest Man

You say you're an honest man
"I can trust you and all that"
Heeded those warning words
Gave my wallet a safe tap

You say you are a nice girl
"We would never part"
Grasped my checkbook tightly
Held on to my heart

You say you're a good customer
But I don't give a rip
Assume you are demanding
Never leave a tip

When you have to say
You're honest, nice, or good
I'm suppose to trust you
But don't think I should

Some People

Some people are divorced
Some people are gay
Others mow their lawn
On the Sabbath Day

Some people relax
A drink or smoke
Others have been known
To tell a dirty joke

Some people are human
So are you
Too bad others don't fit
Your narrow world view

You like to quote the Bible
Think you know what its all about
Re-read the passages on casting stones
The Sermon On The Mount

If you want to reform someone
If you're really that sincere
Why don't you start with the hypocrite
Staring from the mirror

Millenium Georgey

Georgey Porgey kissed a girl
Don't know if he ran away
The teacher kicked him out of school
But, he'll be back someday

Linda offered a friend an asprin
Went against the rules
Got herself expelled
"No drugs in public schools!"

Steve at work said to Nancy
"I really like that dress!"
The boss called him in
Now his life's a mess

Ralph works the night shift
Get shadowed every night
Has to convince the police he's sober
Has his seatbelt on real tight

There are social issues
We need to address
But, its so out of proportion
It's really quite a mess

Where did we lose our focus?
Things have got so bad
If it wasn't kind of scary
It would be funny or just sad

Politically Correct

I think I have it figured out
African-Americans once were black
Indians are now Native-Americans
And they want their land back

Janitors are custodians
Homosexuals are now gay
Mexicans are Hispanic
Anyway, that's what they say

"Happy Holidays" in December
"Merry Christmas" won't do
Better watch what I say
Or I might offend a Jew

I can't walk in their shoes
But try to set things right
Watch every thing I say
Because I'm male, straight, and white

Sixties Syndrome

Admire your determination
Still fighting for change
But many around you view
Your behavior a bit strange

Some may look at you
Say something cruel
"Don't you know long hair is out
Drugs are no longer cool"

"Short hair and patriotism
Have made their return
Social issues have been replaced
By what you have and earn"

The Sixties were exciting
But the Sixties are now gone
Most grey-haired babyboomers
Are just trying to get along

A hippie in the Millenium
No concern for your fate
Keep bucking the system
Like a bull against a gate

While others are complacent
You're fighting to be free
Stuck in Sixties Syndrome
That's where you'll always be

They're Everywhere-They're Everywhere!

You see them on the highway
Spot them in the air
It appears to me
Police are everywhere

Police on motorcycles
Police in cars
Watching people moving
In and out of bars

Cops on horses
Cops on bikes
Surprised I don't see
Tiny cops peddling by on trikes

Poor People

Poor people-poor people
What you going to do
What you going to do?
When they come for you?
Poor people!

Liberal La La Land

Live in Liberal La La Land
Upon a great big hill
Had a minority friend
Back in Graduate School

Admire Reggie and Michael
Find Bill Cosby safe
Avoid them as individuals
Love them as a race

Rented "Dances With Wolves"
Just the other day
Nice to someone at the office
Even though he might be gay

Gave ten dollars
To a charity walk
Greet physically and mentally challenged
With phony baby-talk

Can't comprehend the bigotry
Of the average working man
Perhaps, they're not as smart as me
Just don't understand

Live in Liberal La La Land
Where everything is swell
Behind fences and alarms
Safe inside my shell

My Father's War

They fought on the land
The air and on the sea
Sacrificed so much
To keep our nation free

Immortalized places
Normandy and Bataan
Left their mark stained with blood
Jungle island and desert sand

Some called it "The Good War"
The century's biggest upheavel
Liberated the death camps
Had to stop the evil

Four hundred thousand dead!
What a heavy toll!
Millions more were wounded
Body, heart, and soul

Triumphed over evil
Returned to the U.S.A.
Because of them we now enjoy
A better world today

Now, in their sunset years
Many frail and grey
Thousands pass away before us
Each and every day

Can never repay the debt
But remember what they fought for
The generation that saved the world
Fought in Father's War

Why Do Seniors?

Try to be understanding
Force a patient smile
Watching chatty "blueheads"
Block another aisle

Why do Seniors shop
The busiest time of the day?
Did they always shop this time
Before their spouse passed away?

Or do they get restless
Inside their empty home?
Feel comfort in a crowd
So they don't feel alone?

Part II.

Sentimental Journey

Know Who You Are

Thru these pages
You will see yourself
Know after all this time
You're still the one

Eyes closed-picture you
Touch pillow-feel you
Breathe-your scent
Wet lips-taste you

Thru the corridors
Of my mind
Your footsteps
Still echo

When You Say It

Words on paper
Are small drops of ink
But when spoken, they can be
As careless as Cupids arrows

People often
Throw words around
Especially, that precious
Little phrase

I've seldom used it
Always meant it
What does it really mean?
Is it from the heart?

Do they mean it?
Is it the tequilla talking?
The magic of the moment?
The hormones raging?

So, when you look at me
With puppy eyes
Squeeze my hands
And whisper it

I ask myself
"Girl, what do mean?"
When you whisper
"I love you"

The Moment

Said you never met anyone
Quite like me
Heard it before
But wanted to believe

I said it was the moment
Meant it
Went for it
A surge of crazy passion

Said I made you feel whole
Made you a woman
Hands worked wonders
Mouth-a magical flute

Entwined-we slept
Shallow breathing
Clutching hands
Finally, I pry you away

Instead of elation
Feel dirty and ashamed
Not, because of the moment
When we found each other

But because of the way
I left you to your dreams
Didn't kiss you one last time
Stepped into blinding morning light

Why Can't I?

Why can't I even force myself
To try and talk to you
Why do I ignore you?
What made me act so cruel?

I drive by and see you
Nearly every day
You look for my acknowledgement
But I just turn away

Has pain clouded my compassion?
Do I have too much pride?
Can't accept you as you are?
Bury feelings deep inside?

I doubt you had a sinister plan
To make me feel like a fool
If you never planned to hurt me
Than why must I hurt you?

If I love you as I claim
In a mature and healthy way
Why must I act so cold
As I glance then turn away?

I threw away our friendship
Nurtured through the years
Pretended I no longer cared
Fought back the bitter tears

I can't shape you to suit me
Or turn my feelings of for you
But its still a pathetic excuse
To treat you as I do

I wish you all the happiness
In a life that's not with me
I'll be there if you need me
I'll accept what's not to be

Before You - Since You

Before You

Sullen eyes
Skin pale
Lined face
Feeling frail

Days that were
Endless
Nights that were
Restless

Drinking-smoking
All alone
Hollow nights
Empty home

Ship aground
Spinning down
Life not well
Road to hell

Since You

Happy eyes
Vibrant skin
Learn to laugh
Warm within

Sunshine days
Cheerful-bright
Holding hands
Starry night

Feeling needed
Not alone
Learn to trust
Happy home

Start to heal
Begin to give
Learn to love
Learn to live

Stilted

Stilted conversation
We talk about nothing
No longer laugh
or listen to each other

Bottles clinking
Droning conversations
Jukebox blares
Everything the same, but different

Lost in private thoughts
We silently drown
Know the truth
Fear facing it

You turn toward me
Force a grim smile
Elbow on the bar
I sip my beer

Light a cigarette
Through clouds of smoke
Catch you staring
Into some distant world

Wonder if you're reflecting
On recent dead dreams
Mistakes and regrets
What could have been

Stilted conversation
Mirror our thoughts
In painful silence
Know its over

What Was I Thinking?

What was I thinking?
I'm not a starry-eyed kid
Putting angels on pedestals
Or trying to change someone

Not a guy
Who never had anyone
Became infatuated
Because you showed interest

Then why did I
Fall so hard?
Perhaps, I saw something
Special and beautiful

It was as if
You reached deep down inside
Touched me in a way
I've never been touched

Months turned to years
Fought and denied it
Finally accepted it
Love you like no other

I'm not putting myself down
But, what did I have to offer
Something corny like
I'd try to make you happy?

What was I thinking?
But you know what, my love?
I really thought
I could have pulled it off

The Parking Lot At K- Mart

Could never forget
The time we cut through
The children's section
On the way to sporting goods

Accidently bumped a rack
Of little ruffled dresses
Stood silently-swallowed
You wondered what was wrong

Looked at you painfully
Standing by a row of tiny shoes
Later, you were surprised
Grabbed and kissed you

Took my hand
Pressed it against your stomach
Then "lost it"
In the parking lot at K-Mart

So Sorry

I let her and that
Control my world
Should have buried
Past heartaches

Instead carried
Bitter memories
Knawed heart
Blackened soul

Refused to believe
All women were not
Like her
Took it out on you

The war is history
But it became like
A dirty old knapsack
I refused to discard

My cynisism cut
Deep into you
Everything a joke
Or a game

Trusting no one
Believing in nothing
But quick pleasure
And my own pessimism

You clung on
As I raced to nowhere
Like a hamster
On a wheel

Now, the years
And stress
Haved aged us
Can't change things

Can only say
"I'm so sorry"
You deserved something better
Than a life with me

Some Guy

Don't know whether it was
The road construction
Or a subconscious quirk
That made me drive by

You were sitting on your steps
Head bent down
The way it is
When in deep thought

Running fingers through your hair
Still a beauty
But the clock ticks
The sun sets

Thought about how sad it was
Someone as attractive
And bright as you
Unable to get it together

Some guy might have lifted you
From your rut-filled world
Gave you everything
Loved you for you

You turned and looked
Don't know if you saw me
I didn't honk
Or wave

Wonder what drifted
Through your mind
As you turned and watched
Some guy drive by?

You Are More

You are so unpredictable
You make me want to scream
You're more unstable
Than an NFC football team

More emotional than
A Southern preacher
More temperamental than
A high school music teacher

What is wrong with you?
Can't you be more stable?
Try to steer a steady course?
Find yourself unable?

You have so much to offer
You're a beauty and a brain
Why can't you be more sensible?
Do you have to act insane?

If you get it all together
You'd be something to adore
Men would flock to see you
And, I'd be the first one at your door

Like Number 20

Although you're very different
You're very much alike
Even though you are a woman
He's black and you are white

Tried to get my mind off you
Accept what had to be
Poured myself a beer
Turned on the TV

Thought they could contain him
Succeeded for a time
Rushed in for a tackle
But he charged right through the line

A confusing pile of orange and green
A streak of blue and gray
Did it to them once again
"Old Barry" got away

You are like number 20
No man can pin you down
You feint, jerk, and run
Leave them tumbling to the ground

When You Look At Me

When you look at me that way
You make me feel so sad
When you say you love me
You make me feel so bad

When I say I love you
It tears me up inside
Fearing so much I'll hurt you
Bury the guilt deep down inside

Know where you're coming from
Life's most cruelest game
When we want someone so much
Can't escape the pain

I too know how bad it feels
When things are not to be
For I love someone else
But doubt if she loves me

Don't Cling To Me

The time has finally come
I must be upfront with you
Tell you how I feel
Please don't think me cruel

You may be my friend
And you may be my lover
But, I'm not your little boy
And, you are not my mother

You're a person, not a shadow
Casting images on the ground
You're not a little puppy
So, don't follow me around

No one can save another
Make everything just right
We can only enjoy the moment
So don't cling to me so tight

Please don't get me wrong
I really care about you
I never want to hurt you
Or make you feel a fool

But, I have to have my freedom
You have to let me breathe
If you cling too hard to me
You'll force to make me leave

The Ride

You're at that special age
When youthful bluefire merge
With beauty
And limited experience

Reach over and touch my hand
Can't resist
Pull you into my arms
Taste the honey of your mouth

Run fingers through
The plantinum strands
Sweeping about your shoulders
Breathe in your scent

Know this is wrong
But deep inside me a battle wages
Between my male hormones
And reason and morality

Gently push you away
You look more hurt than angry
Say goodbye with glassy eyes
Swaying body dissappears into the night

Know I did the right thing
But I'll hate myself in the morning
For how I longed to regain my youth
Wrapped in the sweetness of your arms

Did You Ride?

Sweet sage
Permeates the room
"Clear of evil spirits," You claim
"Only good spirits remain"

Snuggle against me
Beneath Indian blankets
Stroke bluish-black hair
You drift off to sleep

But I cannot sleep
For suddenly, you become tense
Heart-hammers
Face transforms

Do the spirits call you back?
A century before?
Big sky and open prairie
Buffaloes and freedom?

Did you ride with Crazy Horse
Pound across the plains?
The blood of Sioux warriors
Pulsing through your veins?

Said A Prayer

Said a prayer for you
Just the other night
But I would never tell you
Didn't think it right

Prayed you're happy where you're at
Things are going well
Hope you steer a steady course
Not plummet down to hell

Pray you can deal
With the pain down deep inside
Know if you ever need me
I'll rush to your side

Don't know if my prayers were answered
But I thought I'd take the time
Only took a moment
Didn't cost a dime

Why Is It?

Why is it?
Someone you care for
Views you as
A good friend?

Someone you're nice to
Reads into it
Expects
A serious relationship?

Why is it?
Someone fun to be with
You wouldn't trust
Across the street?

Someone you can trust
With your heart and credit card
Is about as exciting as
A drive across Nebraska?

Why is it?
Some find the right relationship?
While others search in vain
Die bitter and alone?

Don't Think

Don't think you're a goddess
Please don't get me wrong
Acknowledge you are pretty
Intelligent and strong

Tried to understand
Why I became a love-struck fool
Put so much in words
Wrote so much about you

Loving you at times
Caused a lot of stress
But, you inspired my writing
Now, I celebrate some success

I could take you out to dinner
But if I'm not mistaken
Wouldn't be very wise
Because we both are taken

If I Could Have Met You Sooner

If I could have met you sooner
We could have tasted the air on a fresh summer's day
Or danced beneath a diamond sky
Hand in hand in the park-the rustle of leaves

Watching you tilt your head when you laugh
Bronze swirls like liquid fire upon marble shoulders
Bright eyes charged with energy
Making me melt

To be young and foolish with you
Before life's candle becomes old and twisted
Rejoicing in dreams and youth
If only I could have met you sooner

Sun and RAIN, 1994

The Stranger

I look at you and see a stranger
I've never known you before
The dreams and promises, we once had
Are now left floating on the floor

Meaningless moonbeams distorted by time's river
Mystery-a thing of the past
As we turn away from each other
And stare out into each hollow night

Sun and RAIN, 1994

Finally

Knew it inevitable
Taking chances
Pursuing dreams
Can't blame you

Said you were leaving
I sat in a stupor
Didn't make a scene
Embarass us both

Can't help how I feel
But can control how I act
it was crazy from the start
And, I accept the fact

Didn't need to get emotional
For you already know
My spirit will be with you
Everywhere you go

A Bitter Poem

You are the stuff that screams are made of
You don't complete me
Hate means
Being able to say your sorry

She Smiled

A pretty girl
Smiled at me
Does she like me?
Want to go out with me?

Trying to make someone jealous?
Is she just a flirt?
Gets cruel satisfaction
Seeing guys get hurt?

Does she want to rock my world?
Want to be my wife?
Have my baby
Cause me a lot of strife?

What is the motive
Of this attractive lass?
Maybe she really likes me
Or perhaps its only gas?

Part III.

Love And Family

The Magical Place

You would nestle beside me
A blanket and a stuffed animal
I read you stories about
Princes, castles, and magical places

Every year we would watch
our favorite movie
You would cry everytime
Even though you knew Dorothy made it home

Said I was like him
You would miss me most
Foreshadowed the war drums
Had to leave-missed you most

Could no longer protect you
Be the one stable force
Be the scarecrow
Keep you from harm's way

Returned years later
Had my own problems
Baby sister grown
With problems of her own

By then, we both knew the truth
There is no land of enchantment
No Emerald City or ruby slippers
No way to get back home

There is only the real world
Prisms of light-dark shadows
Sometimes wonderful
Sometimes terrible

On sun-baked days
Frosty mornings
Snowy nights
Still think about it

Could have kept you safe
Innocent and happy
If only there had been
A magical place

Mikey Swings

When Mikey swings
He's really extra sweet
Shakes his tiny fists
Kicks his little feet

Makes adorable cooing sounds
Wiggles baby toes
And when he gets upset
He wrinkles up his nose

And there's that special something
You never want to miss
Bend over and hug him
Get his famous Mikey kiss

When life gets you down
Want to feel good for awhile
Picture Mikey on his swing
Break out in a smile

Why Do People Love Them?

Why do people love them?
One has to wonder why
After all, they like to sleep
And really like to cry

Babies don't say much
Only make a coo
Keep you up at night
Appear to like to drool

But babies are so adorable
Precious and so sweet
Having one around the house
Is really kind of neat

When you pick them up
Hold them to you tight
You think of love and innocence
And everything that's right

Being A Grandparent

Being a grandparent is so wonderful
Because they think you're great
And the feelings more than mutual
Of that, there's no mistake

It makes no difference
If they're girls or boys
You fill them full of junk food
Buy them lots of toys

Get down and play with them
Have a lot of fun
Beam with joy at everything
Your little angels done

And if they need a change
Or act a little bad
You pick them up and hand them
To their mom or to their dad

Give them a farewell hug
As they head out the door
With a bag of goodies
From the one that they adore

Safely in their carseat
Watch them drive away
Knowing that they'll be back real soon
To brighten up a day

Instead Gave Me

Remembered golden days
Spent with your mother
Can't forget how great it was
To be her big brother

She would toddle beside me
We played in the park
Snowmen in the winter
Stories after dark

Years passed by
Had my little boys
Enjoyed special moments
Shared in all their joys

But memories drifted back
To those days long ago
A precious little girl
That I loved so

Then you were born
I could relive it all with you
Read you stories
Took you to the zoo

God must have listened
Put my heart at ease
Didn't give me a daughter
Instead gave me a neice

The Baby Did This

Before you became a father
Conversing with you was fun
But now, you only talk about
What the baby's done

"The baby smiled at me
He's learning to crawl
When he's sleeping
He looks just like a Doll"

Can't you talk about anything
Except what the baby's done?
Is being a father
Really that much fun?

The reason for this call
I had a baby boy
Never been so proud
Never felt such joy

Now, its payback time
The baby did this
The baby did that
So what do you think about that?

You Say

You say that you're leaving me
Heading back to mother
Or did you say
You found yourself a lover

Or did you say the tests came back
Confirmed your worst dread
Better grasp the moment
For you will soon be dead

Or did you say you won the lottery
That we are set for life
More money than we can spend
No more financial strife

Actually, I haven't heard
A single word you said
And if you think I listened
You must have lost your head

Its not that I don't love you
After all, you are my wife
And you certainly are
The most important thing in my life

But when the clock strikes twelve on Sunday
You must leave me alone
For now it's time for me
To enter football twilight zone

House And Not a Home

Bought another jet-ski
To go with the other one
Take it to the river
Have a lot of fun

We only buy brandname clothes
From the most expensive stores in town
Flaunt our fancy garb
Proudly parade around

Eat at four star restaurants
No greasy burgers for my wife
We travel-every winter
Enjoy the best in life

Our house is not a home
But its organized and neat
No toys or baby clothes
Or patter of little feet

The house is really quiet
Except for the TV
An occassional phone call
A disk on the C.D.

The day will come
When we'll store our stuff away
Sitting in our sterile world
When we are old and gray

When it becomes too late
It will become apparent
You can buy a lot of junk
If you don't become a parent

No one will visit us
We will sit here all alone
Because we chose to have a house
And not to have a home

A Message To My Son

I open the door ever so quietly
And gently look inside
I see you sleeping soundly
With a teddy bear by your side

I feel a rush of happiness
That my soul could never hide
You're my son, my little boy
And my heart swells with pride

That lovely face with deep blue eyes
Those outstreched arms that reach for me
The little patter when you walk
The greatest thing there is to me

Everyday I relearn life
And share it all with you
A car, a truck, a train, a squirrel in a tree
The sun, the moon, a bird in flight, a buzzing bumble bee

I want to teach you all
Of life's most pleasant joys
Of books and sports and nature
The world is full of toys

I worry as I watch you grow
Will you always be this way
Or will you turn against me
And break my heart someday

Or worse will you go to war
Armed with knife and gun
And kill or be killed
By someone else's son

But remember no matter what happens between us
In the years to come
You will always be my pride and joy
My hopes, my dreams, my son

Sun and RAIN, 1994

When I Was Young

When I was young
My father stood ten feet tall
When I was a teenager
He didn't know a thing at all

Now, I'm a parent
Try to do my best
But those kids of mine
Really put me to the test

"Because I said so!"
"Because I'm your father!"
"We can't have anything nice!"
"So, why do I bother!"

"Clean up your room!"
"Get off the phone!"
"Turn off those lights!"
"Leave the thermostat alone!"

"When I was your age
"We walked ten miles to school"
"Kids today don't appreciate
A thing their parents do!"

Now, that I'm older
Don't know if its good or bad
But we learned a lot about parenting
Both me and my dad

Part IV.

Alcohol And The Night

Said I Was Your Brother

I was not a hero
But you certainly are
Know where you've been
Know just who you are

Didn't impress the others
Sitting in the bar
Said you had a purple heart
Won the silver star

But I respect you
Know where you're coming from
"Nam" was not a movie
And it really wasn't fun

Said I was your brother
Thought I was real keen
Even though I was a sailor
And you were a Marine

You've been to hell and back
No need to travel far
Relive painful memories
Sitting in a bar

"A Lot Of Questions"

You appear to find me interesting
But I don't know if I should bother
Need to ask a lot of questions
Before I pursue you further

Is that barstool you're sitting on
Reserved in your name?
A drink or two from now
Will you start to act insane?

I don't know how to ask you this
But I think that I should know
Do you play girl's softball?
Is "Ellen" your favorite show?

Have an old boyfriend
In and out of your life?
Is he jealous and obsessive?
Does he own a gun or knife?

Is your life a perpetual crisis?
Always have to play a game?
Because I've had my share of intrigue
And I don't enjoy the pain

Still looking for Prince Charming?
Someone to make things right?
Lady, I'm not Prince Charming
And I doubt that your Snow-White

Need a father for the children?
I find that rather sad
But if I tried to discipline them
"I don't have to you're not my dad!"

I sure do miss the Eighties
Would look at a girl's hand
Knew she was available
Unless she wore a band

One Is Too Many

One is too many
A million not enough
So why do you continue
To pound the stuff?

You're not hurting
Just yourself, you see
Many care about you
Most of all, there's me

There is help available
For others and for you
But you'd rather play denial games
Stay the drunken fool

When you're getting smashed
I see it in your eyes
Then you disappear to binge
Return and tell me lies

You may think everything is normal
Your life is really swell
But the disease is talking to your mind
As you spiral straight to hell

This dangerous course you're on
You know it just won't last
Because one will hurt you slowly
A million will kill you fast

The Stalker

The Ancients knew the stalker
And so do we
He travels on the land
Sweeps across the sea

Brought him to America
Stored in a ship's hold
Traded to the natives
Stole their land and gold

He has many disguises
He's a bottle, he's a can
Seduces lots of women
Is a scourge of man

Some handle the stalker
Relax and have fun
But for others, he's a danger
Beware! You better run!

Marriages in shambles
Children live in fear
Abuse of every kind
Because of booze and beer

There's "A floater" in the river
A string of smashed up cars
Scores of battered women
Fights break out in bars

The stalker racks up victims
Watches people fall
Pushes pain to many
His name is alcohol

Through Our Daughter

Never were a child
Had a happy life
Adrift in a sea of alcohol
Family torn by strife

No wonder you mistrusted
Impulsive-"Do it now!"
"Life is but a lie
"Nothing works anyhow!"

Became what you hated
Tried to shield the pain
Escaped into a bottle
Played the fatal game

You were like an injured bird
Couldn't take off in flight
Met you-learned to love you
Fought to make things right

Wanted to stop the hurt
Kiss away the salty tears
Heal the bleeding wound
Sweep away the fears

Gazed into doleful eyes
The truth you could not hide
Broke down the walls of solitude
Found the beauty deep inside

A peal of happy laughter
Adoring parents-not alone
Anchored in a sea of love
A safe and happy home

Tears of joy
Found the world you never knew
Through our daughter given back
What was stole from you

Let The Monster Sleep

Sometimes, he's not a monster
He's a "Jeckel and a Hyde"
Now, he's had the poison brew
Beware!, Go run and hide

Fortunately for the monster
He did not take the car
Mom is codependent
Drove him from the bar

Smashes through the front door
A real-life psychopath
Screaming incoherent
Hear his obscene wrath

Rush into the closet
The monster's getting near
Hold my little sister
Feel her shake with fear

Hope he doesn't hurt my mom
Crashes up the stair
Stumbles to the bedroom
Retreats into his lair

Trembling hands together
Bow my head and pray
Lord, let him sleep till morning
Make the monster go away

Still Waiting

Noticed you the moment
You walked in the door
You were different than the others
Confident but humble

Didn't appear desperate
Like a dog in heat
Didn't bombard me
With lines of B.S.

I hate to even say it
But you treated me like a lady
You listened to me
Made me laugh

We played with the jukebox
Danced every song
Felt like a teenager
Younger than my daughter

You told me you were tired
Of the bar scene
Kissed me, but said
You wouldn't be back

But I didn't believe you
So I still wait
Same time "Happy Hour"
Same place-third stool from the door

The Roughest Bar In Town

Had to check it out
See what was going down
Wonder why they called it
The roughest bar in town

Read the sign on the door
Thought they must be joking
"Sorry that we're open
Thank you for smoking"

Bikers used to hang here
But thought the patrons tough
Felons used to come here
But thought the place too rough

The so-called music
Made my skin crawl
Had more decibels
Than a chain-saw

The bar reeked of sweat
Cheap booze and stale beer
If you wanted a Manhatten
I doubt you'd get it here

Customers were sprawled
On the bar and floor
Bartenders wouldn't cut them off
If they wanted more

Thought I better make an exit
Before things got too grave
Having more than three teeth
A recent bath and shave

So I climbed over the couple
Lying on the floor
Dodged a couple fist fights
Dashed out of the door

Walking On Eggshells

Turn the TV off
Put away the toys
Turn the CD player down
Don't make any noise

He is very sick right now
Mom told us to be our best
No need to push his buttons
Put him to the test

When he's not this way
He's a husband and a dad
But then something happens
And he starts to act real bad

Mom told us to be forgiving
Someday we'll understand
When someone we love so much
Gets a little out of hand

So we walk on eggshells
Trying to avoid some pain
Be the best till he is well
Daddy's drunk again

Believed You

Said it at the meeting
You were staying off the booze
No more detox
No more antabuse

You gave quite a speech
Made me want to cry
Believed your every word
Thought you wouldn't lie

I can understand slipping
Some do after years
Fall off the wagon
Drink a couple beers

But right after the meeting
I hopped into a car
Drove by a hypocrite
Sneaking into a bar

Looking For A Quiet Place

Tried to find a quiet place
Man, I need a break
Found a cozy bar
Made a big mistake

Could have gone to a biker bar
But wouldn't fit in right
Don't own black clothing
Ride a mountain bike

Could have tried a college bar
Relax and have a beer
Blasting music and little cliques
Shouting the "F" word in my ear

The bar was nearly empty
Ordered myself a drink
Thankful, I found a place
Where I could relax and drink

The calm was soon replaced
By a noisy din
The door swung open
And obnoxious you walked in

Can't give the jukebox a rest
You've played every tune
Must you bang around
Like a drunken loon?

What is wrong with you
Why can't you let things be?
Are you starved for attention?
Are you Adult ADD?

Now, you're shaking for more music
Bashing dice upon the bar
Don't seem to realize
How sickening you are

I'm usually quite mellow
Not a drunken fool
But slam that dice down one more time
I'll knock you off your stool

Whacked Out

Why are you so whacked out?
Why do you act insane?
Is it drugs or alcohol?
A chemical imbalance to the brain?

Was it your homelife
That makes you so wild?
Take a nose-dive out the highchair
When you were just a child?

Did something tragic happen
To make you act this way?
Do you battle demons from the past
Just to make it thru the day?

Understanding all
May make one forgive
But you'll have to change your attitude
If you want to live

Why Do People Drink?

Some people like to party
Have a lot of fun
When they're young and restless
Always on the run

Some drink to celebrate
A promotion or a child
Or some other milestone
So they get a little wild

Others drink heavily
When their life's a temporary mess
Divorce or job loss
Or some other stress

But others have a lot of pain
It tears them up inside
Try to quell the storm
Truths they cannot hide

Little Girl

Little girl with unwashed face
With head bent down and sullen eyes
Your coat is torn, you have no mittens
Your parents ignore your cries

Because mom and dad fight and drink
You're afraid of touch, you tremble so
They ignore your pain, they have their own
Can't see your hurt or feel your woe

Will you ever look in the mirror
And see someone you like?
Will you happily skip rope?
Or even ride a bike?

Can you ever grow up
And have a happy life?
You know nothing but confusion
And family full of strife

A punching bag for others
With rage, they wonder why
They're caught in traps, they can't explain
They drink, abuse, and lie

Little girl, all grown up
With bruises on body, heart and mind
Will you be like mom and dad
Or will you break the bind?

Sailor's Goodbye

He didn't know whether it was the rays of the sun or a sense of being stared at that made him wake up. He rolled over and saw her staring at him, as if he were her prisoner.

"Good morning, Johnny," she said gently.

"Good morning," Johnny said.

He turned away from her and looked at the baby ben clock on the dresser. "I better start getting ready or I'm going to be late," he said briskly.

"Do you have to go so soon," she asked? It sounded like a plea.

"Listen," he said as he put his hands on her shoulder. "The longer we put this off, the worse its going to be, understand?" She nodded weakly. He walked over to the closet, took out his uniform and started to dress. He could hear her sobbing softly, so he turned toward her. She was holding a hankerchief. Her face was lowered. I knew this was going to happen, he thought. All his life he had tried to avoid scenes, but to no avail.

"Are you sure you don't want me to come down to see the ship off?"

No," he replied. "Things are always such a mess, when ships depart. A big mess."

She started to cry again. He walked slowly back to the bed and sat down beside her. He took hold of her hands and pulled her close. She was trembling. It reminded him of a rabbit, he had found in his parents yard, when he was a child. He wanted to have it as a pet, but it stayed in the same place and shook until it died. He stroked her head and whispered, "Its going to be alright, its okay..." He squeezed her limp hands and said softly, "I have to go now."

He stood and started for the door.

"If anything happens to you over there, I'll kill myself," she blurted.

"Nothing is going to happen to me." They embraced.

"I love you," she sobbed.

"I love you too," he lied. She nodded and said softly, "Call me when you get to Hawaii"

"I will," he said, as he closed the door and headed down the hall. He didn't look back.

It was a pleasant ride back to the base. He could smell the ocean. San Diego was a nice city once a person got to know it and one couldn't ask for better weather. By the time he reached the pier, the melodrama had begun, there was even a band. Some people were holding up signs such as, "Goodbye Daddy," and "Good luck U.S.S Meade. There were married men kissing their wives and single men saying farewell to their sweethearts. It looked so sincere and it made him nauseated. Never assume a damn thing, someone once told him and he never forgot.

Everything was chaotic aboard the ship. It appeared a hundred conversations were going on at once.

"Hey, Johnny," a friend called out. "Ready for those girls in Hong Kong?"

"Sure am," he replied with a short laugh.

The band started to play and the dependents started to depart the ship. As the ship began to pull away from the pier, cheers were raised and sailor's threw their hats from the ship to the pier. Johnny noticed a little boy standing alone. He was away from the crowd. Johnny swallowed. He took off his hat and flung it. The hat floated down and the little boy scurried across the pier and grabbed it. Johnny turned away. The lines were off and the ship was picking up speed. It passed the lighthouse on Point Loma and headed to open sea, A gentle breeze began to blow and the ship started to rock. The smell of salt was in the air. She would write and he would probably answer, at least for awhile. He turned and watched the coast of California disappear.

About the Author

Dennis Gibbons was born in Detroit, Michigan. He graduated from the University of Wisconsin – LaCrosse with majors in History and English. He served in the U.S. Navy during the Viet Nam War and also worked with NATO Forces in Northern Europe.

Righteous Reflections is Gibbon's fourth book. *Sun and Rain* is a reflection of the Viet Nam Era. *Thinking of You* is a collection of romantic poetry. *The Light and the Dark* deals with alcohol and the night life.

Gibbons currently lives in Wisconsin, where he is employed as a teacher.

www.ingramcontent.com/pod-product-compliance
Ingram Content Group UK Ltd.
Pitfield, Milton Keynes, MK11 3LW, UK
UKHW041934190726
13854UKWH00004B/1583

9 780759 652361